HOW TO DRAW

POKÉMON ®

by Tracey West

SCHOLASTIC INC.

New York   Toronto   London   Auckland   Sydney
Mexico City   New Delhi   Hong Kong   Buenos Aires

ISBN-13: 978-0-439-43440-9
ISBN-10: 0-439-43440-8

48 47 46   17 18 19 20/0
Printed in the U.S.A.
First Scholastic printing, September 2002

Drawing Pokémon is fun! With the help of this book, you'll learn to draw your favorite Pokémon like a pro. Keep these tips in mind while you work:

*USE A PENCIL!

As you draw, you'll be adding different parts of your Pokémon on top of each other, and you'll have to erase lines you don't need. When you are done, you can go over the important lines with a black marker.

*KNOW YOUR SHAPES!

Many Pokémon might seem impossible to draw, but they're not so hard once you realize that they are often made up of simple shapes such as circles, ovals, and triangles. Check out this Jumpluff, for example. If you can draw circles, you can definitely draw Jumpluff!

*GO AHEAD, COLOR THEM!

Keep an official Pokémon handbook nearby when you're coloring in your drawings. That way you'll get the colors just perfect.

Ready to dive in?
Get your pencil, get some paper, and get drawing!

Height: 1' 00"
Weight: 2 lb

It's easy to see why Igglybuff is called the Balloon Pokémon. Besides being round, Igglybuff's body is very flexible and elastic.

Start with a simple circle. Add two small circles for the eyes, then four curved lines for Igglybuff's tiny hands and feet.

Start adding detail to Igglybuff's eyes. Add its mouth next, and keep it smaller than the eyes. Don't forget to add the poofy shape to the top of Igglybuff's head!

No Igglybuff would be complete without the spiral-shaped curl above its eyes.

Now that you've drawn Igglybuff, see if you can draw its evolved form, Jigglypuff! You'll start with the same simple circle.

CLEFFA™

Height: 1' 00"
Weight: 7 lb

Cleffa's pointy ears and feet give its body a star shape. That's why some people think that Cleffa, like Clefairy and Clefable, traveled to Earth on a meteor.

1

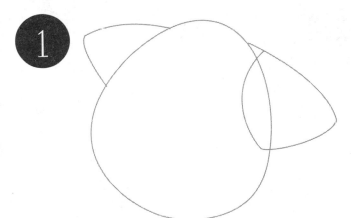

Take away the pointy ears and feet, and Cleffa's body is shaped a lot like an egg. Start by drawing the egg shape, then add two rounded triangles at the top for ears.

2

Cleffa's eyes and cheeks are thin ovals. Add a wavy line for its mouth, and two rounded triangles for hands and a curved line for the tail. Finally, add the feet and the cute curl on top of its head.

3

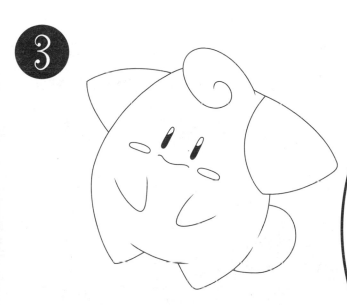

Fill in part of Cleffa's eyes with black, leaving some white on the top. When you're done, make sure you erase any lines you don't need.

To make a smiling mouth, draw a straight line and a curved line.

The leaf growing on top of Chikorita's head gives off a sweet smell, but it can be used in the devastating Razor Leaf Attack.

1

First, draw the outline of Chikorita's body. Then go to the top of the head and draw the leaf. Start with a long, curved line, then add the wavy line underneath.

2

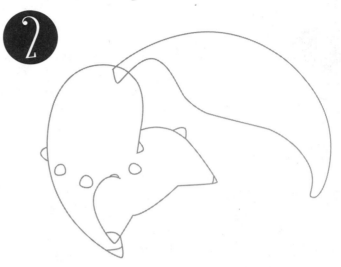

Add a curved line to make Chikorita's front leg, and give Chikorita a rounded triangle for a tail. Finally, add the buttonlike dots that ring Chikorita's neck. They are shaped like gumdrops.

3

Use straight lines to draw Chikorita's eyes. The slants on top of the eyes show that Chikorita is in attack mode.

4

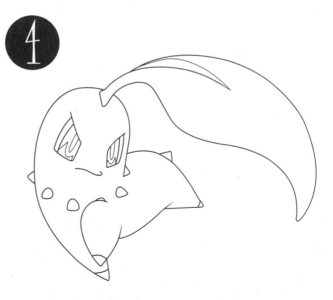

Add detail to the inside of Chikorita's eyes. Erase any outline lines you don't need anymore. Now Chikorita is ready for action!

Those flames shooting out of Cyndaquil's back aren't always there. This Fire Pokémon shoots them when it gets scared or needs to attack. When it's resting, it curls up into a ball.

1 Begin by drawing a perfect circle for Cyndaquil's head. Add a rounded triangle for Cyndaquil's snout. Draw an oval for Cyndaquil's left leg, and add the lines for its body. Then draw the rest of the legs, arms, feet, and the outline of the flames shooting out of its back.

2 Erase the line attaching the head to the snout. Then, add a large curved line for Cyndaquil's eye.

3 Draw more jagged, straight lines inside the flames. Smooth and perfect the shape of Cyndaquil's head, arms, and legs.

4 Erase any extra outline lines. Then stand back! Cyndaquil is one hot Pokémon.

7

TOTODILE ™

Height: 2' 00"
Weight: 21 lb

Totodile looks tough in this pose, but you'll usually find Ash's Totodile laughing, showing off, and having fun.

1

Draw one part of Totodile at a time, following the shapes as best as you can. Start with the head. Add its body and tail. Give Totodile two strong legs and two short arms. Then add the triangle-shaped spikes to Totodile's back and tail.

2

3

8 Add some straight lines to Totodile's chest. Then draw the line of Totodile's long, crooked jaw.

Use this step to make the outline of Totodile's body rounder and smoother. Then finish this step with an outline for a big eye.

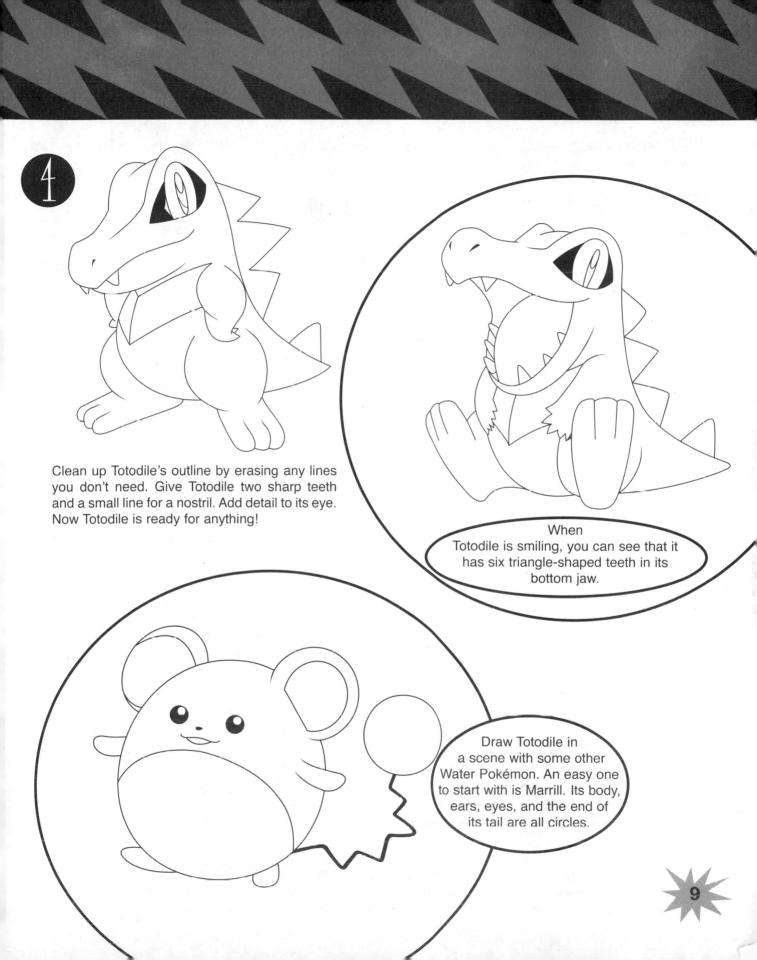

4

Clean up Totodile's outline by erasing any lines you don't need. Give Totodile two sharp teeth and a small line for a nostril. Add detail to its eye. Now Totodile is ready for anything!

When Totodile is smiling, you can see that it has six triangle-shaped teeth in its bottom jaw.

Draw Totodile in a scene with some other Water Pokémon. An easy one to start with is Marrill. Its body, ears, eyes, and the end of its tail are all circles.

9

When Totodile evolves, it becomes Croconaw, the Big Jaw Pokémon. Croconaw is more than a foot taller and 30 pounds heavier than Totodile.

1

Start this tough guy by drawing an egg for its body. Add a snout, arms, and legs. Croconaw gets two triangle-shaped spikes on its back, a crown of jagged lines on its head, and a half-circle for an eye.

2

Give Croconaw a triangle-shaped tail, and follow the picture to draw a line for Croconaw's big jaw.

3

10 Draw the shapes on Croconaw's belly. Then draw five pointy fingers inside the lines for each hand and three toes on each foot. Give its arms and body a more defined shape.

4

Add two sharp, triangular teeth poking out of its jaw, and a diamond-shaped spike to the end of its tail. Finally, erase any extra lines. That's quite a Croconaw you've drawn!

WOBBUFFET™

Jessie from Team Rocket accidentally traded her Lickitung for a Wobbuffett. Her new Pokémon has a habit of popping out of its Poké Ball when it's not wanted.

1

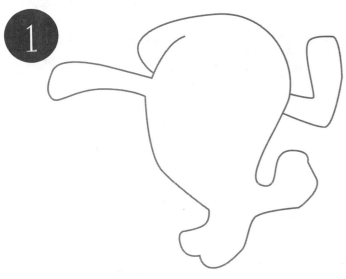

This Wobbuffet is jumping for joy, so its basic body shape leans toward the right. Add feet and arms. Make sure the arm pointing up is not higher than Wobbuffet's head.

2

To draw a perfect smile on Wobbuffet, make a large letter "U" just slightly above the middle of its body. Top it with a jagged line and add a curved line on the inside for a tongue. Before moving on, add a flat teardrop-shaped tail.

3

Erase any lines you don't need. Draw lines for Wobbuffet's eyes, and don't forget the pattern on its tail.

Wobbuffet is one of several Pokémon with unusual tails. Can you draw Girafarig's tail?

PIKACHU™

Height: 1' 04"
Weight: 13 lb

Ash's Pikachu has been his companion ever since Ash started his Pokémon journey. Pikachu is awfully cute, but as everyone knows, you don't want to mess with its electric attacks!

1

From top to bottom, Pikachu's head is about the same size as its body. Remember that, and you'll have a top-notch Pikachu.

2

Where would Pikachu be without its lightning-bolt-shaped tail? Use straight lines to draw the tail peeking out from behind its body.

3

Give Pikachu five tiny fingers on each hand and three toes on each foot. The lines on Pikachu's ears show where the yellow ends and the black tips begin.

12

4

Erase the extra outlines. Add two circles for Pikachu's cheeks. Make sure the circles are attached to the side of the face.

5 Give Pikachu a smiling mouth. Then add two circles for eyes. Make sure they are smaller than the circles for Pikachu's cheeks, and try not to draw them too close together.

6 Draw two smaller circles inside the eyes for pupils. Leave these white, and color in the rest in black. Draw a small mark for a nose and fill in the black tips of Pikachu's ears. Finally, add detail to Pikachu's tail. *Awww.* Don't you just want to give it a hug?

7 When Pikachu uses Thunderbolt, lightning flies from its body. Try adding some lightning bolts like these to your Pikachu drawing.

Now that you've gotten the hang of drawing Pikachu, why not try drawing Pikachu in other poses?

PICHU TWINS ™

Height: 1' 00"
Weight: 4 lb

These mischievous twin Pichu showed Pikachu the town in *Pikachu and Pichu in the Big City.* One fun-loving Pichu can be a real handful, but two — well, that's double trouble!

Don't worry — drawing the Pichu twins won't be twice as hard as long as you start simply. Begin by drawing the two oval heads, making sure they overlap. Then add the bodies. Finish this step by using simple lines to add the arms and feet.

You might be tempted to draw triangles for Pichu's ears, but if you look closely you'll see each one is a diamond shape. The bottom point of the diamond is attached to Pichu's head.

Add detail to the Pichu bodies by drawing jagged lines underneath their heads. When you color in your Pichu, these areas will be black.

Add definition to the arms and feet. You'll notice that Pichu hands look like mittens.

5 Erase any extra lines then add detail to the ears. And don't forget the tuft of hair on the Pichu on the right. That's the only way to tell the Pichu twins apart!

6 Make sure the circles for their cheeks are touching the outline of each face. Give each Pichu one eye, and make sure it's smaller than the cheek circle underneath it. Then draw a happy mouth on each face.

7 Use lines to give each Pichu a winking eye and one tiny nose. Add a line to each mouth, giving each Pichu a tongue. Then fill in the black areas on the Pichu's ears, tails, bodies, and eyes. What do you think? These Pichu are just *two* cute!

Making a perfect Pichu is all about proportion. The key is that Pichu's head is twice the size of its body from top to bottom. And each of Pichu's ears is as tall as its head. It's a wonder Pichu doesn't topple over!

TOGEPI™

Height: 1' 00"
Weight: 3 lb

Like Igglybuff and Cleffa, Togepi is one of the Pokémon you'll find in the Johto Region. Misty usually carries her Togepi in her arms, but Togepi often wanders away and stumbles into all kinds of adventures.

Start with a perfect circle. Follow the drawing to add the ridges on top of Togepi's head. Then add two gumdrop-shaped arms and two oval feet.

Just above Togepi's arms, draw the jagged line that shows where Togepi's eggshell cracked when it was hatched. Then draw the outlines of the shapes that decorate the shell.

Begin this step by erasing any lines at the top of the circle that you don't need. Add a smile just above the eggshell, and make sure it's positioned underneath the center point on the head. Finally, add details.

4

Togepi's eyes are two thick half-circles. Add detail to Togepi's mouth. To finish this happy Togepi, erase the extra lines on its feet.

Can you draw Togepi's eyes open? See how easy it is to change its expression?

Now that you've drawn three baby Pokémon, why not try another one on your own? To draw Hoppip, start with a circle shape for its body. Then add arms, feet, ears, and the leaves on its head. Of course, don't forget its smiling face!

Uh-oh! It looks like Meowth is scared of something. Maybe it just heard that Team Rocket is out of food again. Knowing Meowth, it will do whatever it takes to get something yummy in its tummy.

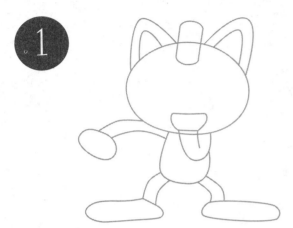

Start with a sideways oval for Meowth's head. Add a body, arms, legs, hands, and feet. Meowth's ears are shaped like rounded triangles. Don't forget the jewel in the center of its head. It is shaped like a rectangle with rounded corners.

Now give Meowth a tail. Notice how the tail starts where Meowth's body and leg meet.

Round out the shape of Meowth's hands and feet. Then draw whiskers on the sides and top of its head — six whiskers in all.

Give Meowth some toes and fingers on its paws and erase any extra lines. Add detail to the jewel and tail. Finally, give Meowth a wavy line for a mouth. Make sure it is curved down to give him a worried look.

5

Draw two pointy triangle teeth, then draw the eyes. As you can see, they are not perfect circles, but more like rounded diamonds.

6

Finish up Meowth by adding details to its eyes. Color in the black part on its ears. You've drawn Meowth — that's right!

What is scaring Meowth? Maybe it's a spooky Ghost Pokémon! Try drawing some Ghost Pokémon next to Meowth. Gastly is basically a circle with big half-circles for eyes. Haunter and Gengar start with circle shapes, too.

Many Pokémon have detailed eyes, just like Meowth. Here is a breakdown of Meowth's "scared" eye:

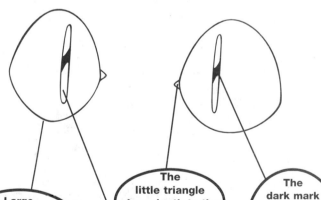

Large, rounded eyeballs are common in many Pokémon.

This part of the eye, the iris, is a long, thin oval. A Pokémon with a happy expression might have a larger, rounder iris.

The little triangle gives depth to the eye shape.

The dark mark in the iris is the pupil. Sometimes, the iris is white.

19

HOUNDOUR™

You're lucky this Houndour isn't chasing you! These combination Dark/Fire Pokémon are fast, fierce hunters. Of course, that doesn't mean they are bad Pokémon — just really tough opponents.

1

Drawing Houndour in motion can be a real challenge. Start by drawing the lines of its body and its right legs. Then add the head, ears, and tail. Take it easy and draw one shape at a time.

2

Now draw Houndour's left legs. They are behind its body, so Houndour's head and right legs overlap them.

3

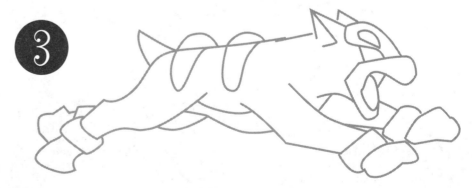

The ridges on Houndour's back make it look tough, but they are easy to draw. Finish this step by drawing an eyebrow above Houndour's eye.

4

Add detail to Houndour's paws and chest. Give it a triangle-shaped nose and two sharp teeth.

5

This Houndour looks like it is ready for battle. Why not create your own Pokémon battle scene with this Houndour? Combine it with the Ursaring on page 25, then stand back and see which of these Pokémon is tougher.

Houndour evolves into Houndoom. Have your drawing skills evolved enough so that you can give Houndoom a try?

21

GYARADOS™

When sailors hear the name "Gyarados," they shudder in fear. This combination Water/Flying Pokémon could break a ship to bits with its powerful snakelike body.

1

Draw long, curved lines to form Gyarados's body. Make sure the body gets thicker as you get closer to the head. Add a fin on the end of its tail. Gyarados has a strange, hammer-shaped head, so do the best you can by following the shape in the drawing.

2

Draw fins on the back of its neck, the bottom of its tail, and the sides of its face. Use thick, curved lines to add those tentacles on either side of its mouth. Then draw the three-pronged crest on its forehead.

3

Take a look at the fin on the end of the tail. See how its end is made up of curved ridges? Fix the fin, and then draw the segments that make up its body. When you're done, give Gyarados a long, wide-open mouth.

22

④

Add more detail to the tail and erase any lines you don't need. Then go back to the head and add eyes, lips, and four triangle teeth in the corners of the mouth.

⑤

Color in the mouth, but leave a white rectangle for its tongue. Then draw lines through the center of each body segment. Gyarados is looking pretty scary already!

⑥

At this stage, you'll be adding some small lines that do a lot to make Gyarados look ferocious. Add nostril lines, and more detail to the tail and head. Finally, draw an oval shape on each body segment. Your Gyarados is sure to make a splash in the Pokémon world!

URSARING™

Height: 5' 11"
Weight: 277 lb

What do you get when a cuddly Teddiursa evolves? Ursaring! When it's hungry, this superstrong Pokémon snaps trees in half and eats the fallen berries off the ground.

Start to draw Ursaring by using strong, straight lines to make its basic body shape. Then follow the drawing closely to make the shape of Ursaring's arms and head.

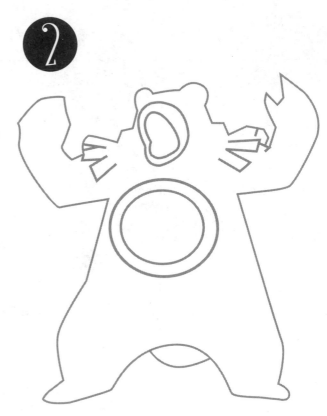

The big yellow circle on Ursaring's chest makes this Pokémon easy to spot. After you draw it, add a wide-open mouth and draw the details on Ursaring's shoulders.

Ursaring's eyes have simple, straight black lines for pupils. Color in the nose and the diamond-shaped marks. Finish up with some sharp teeth, and you've got one frightening Ursaring on your hands. Can you bear to look?

While many Pokémon have fingers, Ursaring has five sharp claws on each hand and three on each foot. When you're done drawing them, start adding details to Ursaring's face. And don't forget to draw the diamond-shaped marks on its paws.

After you've mastered Ursaring, drawing its pre-evolved form should be a piece of cake. To draw Teddiursa, use lots of circles and ovals.

LuGIA™

Height: 17' 01"
Weight: 476 lb

In *Pokémon the Movie 2000,* Ash's friend Melody plays her flute to call forth Lugia from the depths of the ocean. You don't have to play the flute to bring Lugia to life — just use your pencil!

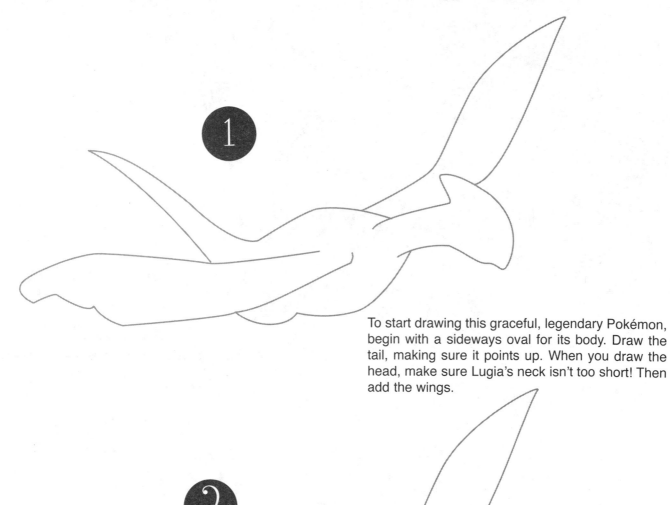

To start drawing this graceful, legendary Pokémon, begin with a sideways oval for its body. Draw the tail, making sure it points up. When you draw the head, make sure Lugia's neck isn't too short! Then add the wings.

Start adding detail to the end of the tail, the chest, and the face. Don't forget to add the outline of feet on the bottom of Lugia's body.

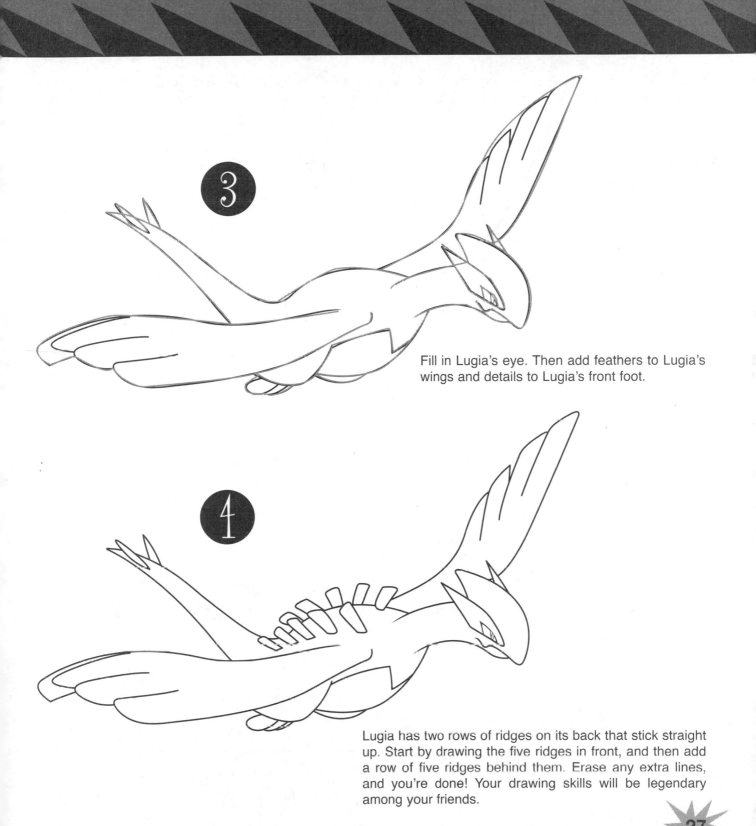

3

Fill in Lugia's eye. Then add feathers to Lugia's wings and details to Lugia's front foot.

4

Lugia has two rows of ridges on its back that stick straight up. Start by drawing the five ridges in front, and then add a row of five ridges behind them. Erase any extra lines, and you're done! Your drawing skills will be legendary among your friends.

27

ENTEI™

Height: 6' 11"
Weight: 437 lb

In the movie *Spell of the Unown*, one of Ash's biggest challenges was battling Entei. Drawing this Volcano Pokémon is a challenge, too, but by this point you have mastered the skills to do it. Don't let your temper erupt — stick to the steps and you'll do great!

1

The key is to remember that Entei is made up of lots of straight lines and sharp angles. Start by drawing Entei's face. Then draw the long, spiky fur around its face. Draw Entei's chest, and then its legs. Finish this step by drawing the outline of the spikes on its back.

2

Entei has a long flowing mane that starts at the top of its head, flows behind its spikes, and curls like a tail behind it. Draw the mane, and then add detail lines to the legs and face.

3

Use this step to make Entei look shaggy. Draw lines of shaggy fur on Entei's legs, chest, mane, and around its face.

④

Erase the lines you don't need anymore. Then add detail lines to give depth to the spikes on Entei's back.

⑤

Add lines to Entei's eyes and details to its mane. See those rings around Entei's legs? You'll need to add some lines to the two right legs, to show dimension.

⑥

A few more lines of detail around Entei's face give it a fierce look. Add lines for pupils, and as a finishing touch, four sharp teeth. Then pat yourself on the back. You've challenged Entei — and emerged successful!

This Fire-type Pokémon is well known for blazing hot attacks, such as Flamethrower and Fire Blast. Why not try drawing Entei hurling flames at an opponent?

In the world of Pokémon, you won't find better friends than Ash and Pikachu. They have been through a lot together! You're sure to have fun drawing these Poké Pals!

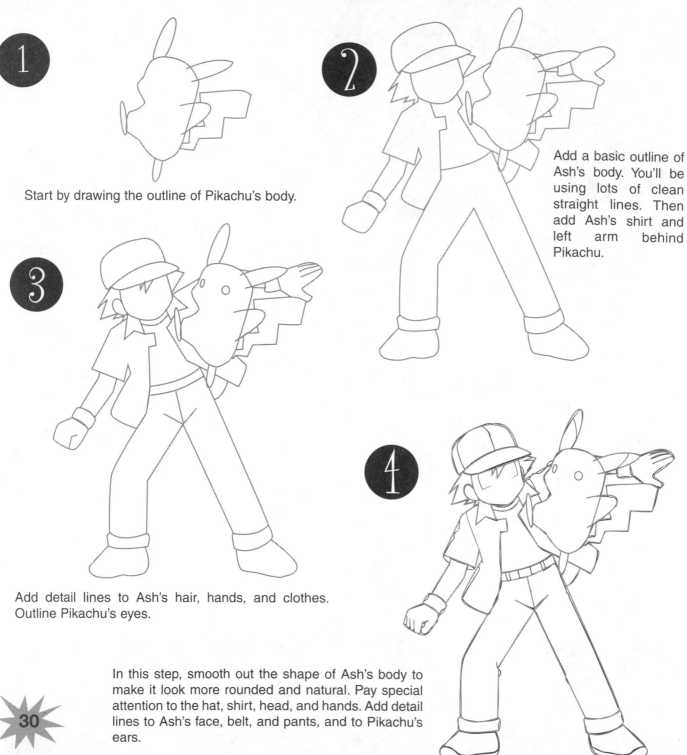

1 Start by drawing the outline of Pikachu's body.

2 Add a basic outline of Ash's body. You'll be using lots of clean straight lines. Then add Ash's shirt and left arm behind Pikachu.

3 Add detail lines to Ash's hair, hands, and clothes. Outline Pikachu's eyes.

4 In this step, smooth out the shape of Ash's body to make it look more rounded and natural. Pay special attention to the hat, shirt, head, and hands. Add detail lines to Ash's face, belt, and pants, and to Pikachu's ears.

30

5 Erase any lines you don't need anymore. Give Ash and Pikachu "U"-shaped mouths. See how Ash's mouth touches the bottom of his chin?

6

Step 6 is all about adding detail lines to make the picture complete. Pay close attention to Ash's belt, pants, and shirt. Draw lines on his fingers to indicate the gloves on his hands. And of course, Pikachu needs those circles for cheeks!

7

Just a few finishing touches! Ash's clothes, shoes, and hat need things like buttons, pockets, and laces. Draw in their eyes, and don't forget those two little "Z"s on Ash's cheeks. Great job! Now Ash and Pikachu are ready for their next adventure.

ASH'S TEAM

Now that you've drawn Ash and Pikachu, why not try drawing them with some of their favorite Pokémon? Start with Ash and Pikachu in the middle of your page. Then add one Pokémon at a time. See if you can spot basic shapes in the Pokémon, and draw those first. Then keep adding details and erasing extra lines as you go.

   Don't let your drawing adventures stop with this book. Try drawing *your* favorite Pokémon on your own. Who knows? You might find that being a Pokémon artist is almost as fun as being a Pokémon trainer!

Color 'em all!